The Trampoline Machine

by Sascha Goddard

illustrated by Clara Soriano

Chapter 1	Bored at home	2
Chapter 2	A new game	6
Chapter 3	The circus	10
Chapter 4	Outer space	14
Chapter 5	The rainbow volcano	18

OXFORD
UNIVERSITY PRESS
AUSTRALIA & NEW ZEALAND

Chapter 1

Bored at home

It was midway through the school holidays, and Isabel and Ed were stuck at home. They were *so* bored.

They had played all their games and read their new books. They had even watched every episode of their favourite television show, *Crazy Cooking Creations* – twice!

"I only have to work until lunchtime," said Dad. "Then we can go on a bike ride together."

"That's ages away," Ed complained.

"I'm hungry," said Isabel. "Can we eat something?"

"You just finished your cereal!" Dad exclaimed, laughing.

"Go and get some fresh air." He ushered them outside.

Isabel and Ed looked at each other.

"Should we bounce on the trampoline?" Isabel asked hopefully.

She loved the trampoline, but they *had* jumped on it a lot lately.

"I suppose so," shrugged Ed. "I don't have any better ideas."

Chapter 2

A new game

Ed followed Isabel as they climbed up the ladder, through the net and onto the bouncy mat.

Isabel did a few small jumps while Ed lay on his back, staring at the fluffy white clouds.

"Hey, that cloud looks like a penguin," said Ed.

Isabel joined him. "And that elephant cloud is headed right at it," she laughed. "Watch out, penguin!"

Ed chuckled. Then, pointing in another direction he said, "That's an acrobat cloud, and it's doing a backflip."

That gave Isabel an idea.

"Hey, Ed," Isabel whispered. "Want to know a secret?"

Ed was not impressed, but Isabel went on anyway. "See this circle in the middle of the trampoline?" she said. "It's actually the button that operates ... The Trampoline Machine!"

"The what?" said Ed, screwing up his face.

"Come on, Ed. Use your imagination," said Isabel. "What if this trampoline could take us anywhere we wanted to go? And all we have to do is name the place and touch the button."

Suddenly, Isabel slammed her hand down on the circle, shouting, "The circus!"

Chapter 3

The circus

Ed looked down – he was wearing a colourful acrobat costume. Isabel was up high, swinging from a trapeze. Suddenly, she let go, bounced on the trampoline and did a somersault through the air.

"Listen to the crowd cheer," shouted Isabel with excitement. Ed grinned and started bouncing.

"Watch me perform my incredible triple backflip," he shouted.
Ed jumped as high as he could, then backflipped three times.
He landed perfectly, holding his arms high.

"Woo!" shouted Isabel, rolling with laughter as she reached for the circle.

"Ready?" she asked, grinning. "Next stop – outer space."

Chapter 4

Outer space

Isabel floated past Ed in her shiny silver spacesuit.

"Wow," said Ed, soaring across the trampoline. "We hardly weigh anything. It's like we can fly."

"Ed, this is serious," said Isabel, winking at him. "We're astronauts on an important mission."

"Oh, right," Ed replied, winking back. "We must get to the mysterious location on the moon, without being captured by the space villain."

Just then, the spaceship jerked. Ed and Isabel were thrown to the right. They bounced around everywhere.

"It's the villain!" shouted Isabel. "He bumped our ship with his and we've gone off course."

Quickly, she grabbed the controls, pushed them up to full speed and carefully steered the ship to their destination.

"Phew," said Ed, breathing a sigh of relief. "Isabel, you are a space hero."

Isabel grinned proudly.

"Now," Ed continued, with a cheeky smile, "let's get out of here."

With that, Ed pushed hard on the button, saying loudly, "*Crazy Cooking Creations!*"

Chapter 5

The rainbow volcano

Isabel looked around at the bright lights and television cameras. She and Ed wore orange aprons and white chef hats. In front of them was the craziest cooking creation they had ever seen.

A brown mountain with rough edges rose up from the table. Small bits of honeycomb were stuck all around it. Out of the top gushed a fountain of colourful icing.

"What on earth is this thing?" Isabel exclaimed, giggling.

"No idea," replied Ed. "But we have to finish making it before that timer goes off – in 30 seconds!"

"Wait," said Isabel. "I know – it's a rainbow volcano."

"Right," said Ed. "Let's finish the rainbow lava. It needs to run down the sides like a real volcano."

Isabel bounced to the top shelf where the coloured icing sat and grabbed the tubes.

"Are you ready?" she shouted. "Here come the yellow, red, blue, green, pink, purple and orange."

One by one, she threw them down to Ed.

Ed quickly opened the tubes. They put the
icing next to the cake and squeezed hard.

Long lines of colour shot out and swirled
down the sides of the chocolate mountain.

Their creation looked incredible – *and* crazy!

Ding, ding, ding, went the timer.

"We did it!" said Isabel, jumping super high on the trampoline.

"High-five!" said Ed. "Hey," he added, "are you hungry?"

Isabel grinned, and they raced inside.

Dad walked into the kitchen just as they started pulling out boxes and jars. "What's happening here?" he asked, smiling.

"Sorry, Dad," said Isabel. "We don't have time for that bike ride after all."

"Why not?" asked Dad, surprised.

"Well," said Ed, "it takes a while to make a rainbow volcano."